Easy Transfers

ROCKPORT

First published in the United States of America by
Rockport Publishers, Inc.
33 Commercial Street
Gloucester, Massachusetts 01930-5089
Telephone: (978) 282-9590
Fax: (978) 283-2742
www.rockpub.com

ISBN: 1-56496-851-0

10 9 8 7 6 5 4 3 2 1

Design and Cover: Kathryn Sky-Peck
Photography: Bobby Bush Photography
Illustrations: Lorraine Dey
Layout: Leeann Leftwich Zajas

Printed in China

Easy Transfers
for Any Surface

CRAFTING WITH IMAGES AND PHOTOS

Livia McRee

GLOUCESTER MASSACHUSETTS

ROCKPORT PUBLISHERS

Contents

6   **INTRODUCTION**

8   Finding Artwork

10   Modifying Art by Hand and Computer

14   **TRANSFERS TO FABRIC**

16   Techniques and Tips for Fabric Transfers

18   Memory Art Canvas

22   Commemorative Collage Pillow

26   Indian Folk Art Bag

30   Indonesian Table Runner

34   **TRANSFERS TO WOOD**

36   Techniques and Tips for Wood Transfers

38   Border-Framed Mirror

42   Illustrated End Table

46   Faux-Painted Clock

50   Family Tree

54 TRANSFERS TO STONE AND POROUS SURFACES

56 Techniques and Tips for Stone and Porous Surface Transfers

58 Stone Tile Coasters

62 Faux Porcelain Plaster Box

66 Terra-Cotta Pots

70 Saltillo House Number Plaque

74 TRANSFERS TO POLYMER CLAY

76 Techniques and Tips for Polymer Clay Transfers

78 Pendant and Pin Set

82 Tiled Backsplash

86 Matisse Kitchen Magnets

90 Suncatcher Mobile

94 **GALLERY OF ART FOR PROJECTS**

112 **RESOURCES**

115 **ABOUT THE AUTHOR**

116 **ACKNOWLEDGMENTS**

Introduction

Transfer technology opens up an exciting realm of possibilities. Any image—from a photograph of a baby to an antique illustrated fruit-crate label—can be transferred to just about any surface. This merging of crafts and graphic design is an ideal way to create beautiful, personal items for home decoration and gift giving.

The possibilities for transfer projects are expansive. They include making original artwork using pressed and dried flowers to decorate a refreshing linen table runner, using an intricate Chinese painting to decorate a sumptuous satin pillow, molding translucent polymer clay suncatchers decorated with colorful, hand-painted artwork, and creating a set of stone coasters decorated with retro illustrated advertisements. Transfer technology is improving and expanding all the time, and new techniques are just waiting to be discovered and explored.

Numerous clip art books are now available that offer every conceivable style and kind of art, copyright free, to everyone. From Japanese geometric designs to art nouveau paintings, clip art is a great way to incorporate gorgeous images into a craft project. Clip art can also be used as a starting point or reference for creating original artwork. Personal photographs are another wonderful source for transferred images. Photos can provide unique and interesting art, especially when manipulated with simple image-editing software for the home computer.

This book is intended to be a helpful manual for exploring the art of transferring. Each chapter focuses on a different material onto which images may be transferred and contains a Techniques & Tips section for troubleshooting and easy reference. Use this information as a guideline for working with particular techniques and surfaces, but always experiment and don't be afraid to bend the rules. Above all, have fun.

Finding *Artwork*

Seek out artwork for crafting with transfers the same way a graphic designer would hunt down an image for a professional assignment. A trip to the art-technique section of a bookstore, a visit to an on-line stock image archive, or a spin through a CD-ROM image collection can result in some great finds.

CLIP ART

Clip art is a generic term for copyright-free images, such as illustrations, borders, and backgrounds, that were created for commercial or decorative purposes and are now compiled into books or on CD-ROMs, available for use in new works. The style and variety of available clip art is staggering—from 1930s illustrated advertisements to cigar box labels, Indian textile prints to Celtic illuminated borders. This "recycled" artwork is a staple for graphic artists and transfer artists alike.

Large bookstores usually have sections dedicated to the subject of art technique. It is usually in this section that clip art books can be found. Many books are packaged with a CD-ROM, which contains professional scans of all of the book's artwork. This is not only timesaving, but also enables anyone with a printer and computer—but no scanner—to work digitally. See Resources on page 112 for information on clip art publishers.

ON-LINE STOCK IMAGE PROVIDERS

Browse thousands of images by keyword with on-line stock image providers. Enter a keyword or two, click a button, and all the corresponding images in the database will pop up on a virtual light board. A digital watermark on the images indicates copyright protection. Many on-line stock image providers only cater to the professional market and charge hundreds of dollars for one image. However, for a few dollars, a company called Corbis (www.corbis.com) will allow images to be downloaded for non-commercial use. In other words, use them freely to make gifts and home decorating projects, but don't open up a store to sell the crafts.

MAKING IMAGES

Personal and family photos, children's drawings, pressed leaves and flowers, scraps of old paper, fabric, and just about any other fairly flat material can be used to make images for use in transfer projects. Start thinking of new ways to combine such materials to create collages for projects. Ticket stubs or interesting receipts from a memorable trip layered around a photo can creatively capture the essence of time spent with friends or family. Transfer this image to a canvas or a box top for a truly special, personal craft.

WHAT'S FREE TO USE?

Since copiers and scanners make it so easy and appealing to duplicate images, copyright concerns have become increasingly prevalent. For the craftsperson and artist, it's often tricky to determine what can be duplicated freely and what restrictions, if any, apply to that use. Here are a few things to take note:

· Some, but not all, copyrighted works are marked with the copyright symbol—©. Keep in mind that photographs are copyrighted by the photographer unless otherwise specified in writing. All published materials, including images from magazines and books, are also copyrighted.

· It is a common misconception that scanning a copyrighted image and then slightly changing it using image-editing software is a way to circumvent copyright restrictions, but this is not the case. In fact, it is viewed as destroying the integrity and value of the original work and can result in additional penalties. It is perfectly acceptable, though, to use an image as reference to create an original work.

· Copyrights do expire, and published materials more than fifty years old fall into the public domain unless the copyright is renewed. The drawing on a store receipt that has been out of business for one hundred years is most likely safe to use, but a photo in an old book that's been recently reprinted is not.

· Many copyrighted images can be used with permission. Call or write to the company or publisher that owns the image and describe how the image will be used. To be safe, be sure to get permission in writing. Send a self-addressed, stamped postcard with a sentence or two that grants permission for the use of a specific image. Then all the recipient needs to do is sign and return the card.

· While copyright laws and restrictions can be disheartening, remember that they are in place to protect the creators of images—including you. To officially copyright an original image of your own, simply place your name, the © symbol, and the year on the work. Then write to the Copyright Office, Library of Congress, Washington, D.C. 20559, requesting a form to register the copyright for a small fee.

· When in doubt, play it safe. There are plenty of copyright-free sources for images—starting in the Gallery of Art for Projects section of this book.

Modifying Art *by* Hand and Computer

The artwork for transfers can be prepared by hand using traditional methods or by computer using image-editing software. Both ways will yield gorgeous results. The most important thing to remember is that the quality of the final image will be no better than the original—whether working by hand or on a computer. And, since virtually anything flat can be scanned or copied, there's no limit to the kinds of images that can become a transfer.

BY HAND

When preparing artwork by hand, it is usually necessary to have several copies of the same image. For example, to make the table runner on page 30, first make color copies of the butterfly artwork several times and in several sizes. Then, cut each butterfly out and mount them on a piece of white cardstock using spray adhesive. This way, only one piece of precious transfer paper is necessary for the project. The rigidity of cardstock will help prevent the images from wrinkling or peeling off by accident, and the spray adhesive provides a smooth, even bond that will minimize the shadows that can appear when copying a piece of layered paper. Since color copies can get expensive, do all design work using a black-and-white copier. Determine all copying percentages before using a color copier.

Try modifying artwork directly by using colored pencils and paint, or splice together patterns to create borders, like the one used in the mirror project on page 38. Heat transfer sheets can also be drawn on before the image is ironed in place; just be sure not to scratch through to the paper beneath—unless that's the desired effect.

USING COLOR COPIERS

Color copies can be used to do many of the same things that image-editing software does, including drastic or minimal color adjustments and image reversals. The best way to learn what a color copier can do is to experiment with one at a shop that sets aside a few machines for self-service.

Since color copying machines are extremely expensive—and using ink jet transfer paper in a color copier will cause major damage—be sure to bring heat transfer paper in its original packaging to the shop. That way, the clerk can be sure that the paper will not ruin the copier. It's also a good idea to ask the local copy shop what kind of copier it has, then purchase papers that specify compatibility with that type of machine. Some copy shops also supply transfer paper.

BY COMPUTER

In order to create and print out transfers by computer, a scanner and image-editing software will be necessary. First and foremost, read the manuals for both thoroughly and follow the recommendations made for specific types of images or effects, such as black-and-white images, printer resolutions, and so on.

SCANNING IMAGES

A decent, easy-to-use flatbed scanner can be purchased for seventy-five to one hundred dollars. It is a fantastic, inspiring tool that transforms an ordinary computer into a remarkable crafting tool. Since color copies can be one to two dollars each, a scanner is a cost-effective investment for the transfer artist.

Basically, scanners need to be told what is being scanned and how to scan it. Is it a photo or a magazine print? What size should it be? Is it in color or black and white? Don't worry. The scanner's software will create an interface that will ask all these questions, so it is simply a matter of checking the right box.

The resolution of the image is another important scanning element that needs to be selected. Resolution is referred to as dpi, or dots per inch. These dots translate into color when the image is printed, and the more dots there are, the sharper and more detailed the image. *For the projects in this book, 150 dpi is sufficient; files with high resolutions take up a lot of memory on a computer and will slow it down.*

IMAGE EDITING

Some scanners are sold with very basic image-editing software, which is great for being introduced to the whole process. But for less than one hundred dollars much more sophisticated programs, such as Adobe Photoshop Elements, provide an intriguing tool. Based on the original Adobe Photoshop, which is an expensive and complex program used by professionals, Elements provides a startling array of possibilities for modifying artwork with an intuitive and fun-to-use interface. For example, a scanned photo can be turned into a watercolor image with literally the touch of a button.

Tip:

When working with a digital file, save it frequently under different names throughout the design process. Then, it will be easy to go back to a certain point and start from there. It also encourages experimentation, since there is no need to worry about ruining the one and only version of an image. As with any work on a computer, it's always a good idea to save often.

The best thing about image editing on a computer is speed. Lighten a dark photo, erase unwanted areas, add a background color—all these changes can be made quite easily and quickly. It's also a snap to change the size or color of an image, make several copies of it, and rotate it in any direction.

PRINTING

Good color printers can also be purchased for less than one hundred dollars. The ink, however, is fairly expensive; so when printing out test sheets, select the economy mode, which uses less ink. Always run a test on a piece of paper before printing on a transfer sheet. There are often details that need to be adjusted, even when everything looks fine on the computer screen. For example, a horizontal document needs to be printed on landscape mode or the image will get cropped. This is something that's very easy to forget, and there are no visual clues until the document is printed. Finally, it's best to load transfer sheets one at a time, and print them one by one. Since they are different in thickness and consistency than standard paper, they can jam printers if several pages are loaded at once.

Transfers *to Fabric*

Fabric is the traditional surface for transfers, so photos and art-work can be integrated into just about any sewing project, from table runners to pillows. The possibilities are seemingly end-less. With so many methods and products now available specially formulated for fabric, it's easy to create distinctive transfers that suit a project perfectly. As for those who don't sew, don't be intimi-dated. There are many ways to craft with fabric without sewing a stitch. Experiment with the techniques described in this book to discover the qualities of each. Transfers can be glossy or matte, trans-parent or opaque, stiff or flexible, and each finish coveys a different mood and style. Combine different types of fabrics with various transfer techniques—not only to determine what works best, but also to make new and interesting discoveries. And always use an appropriate iron setting for the fabric, even if the transfer method suggests a higher heat setting. When working with fabric, remember that the smoother and finer it is, the more completely the image will transfer. Coarser material, such as linen, can also be used but the image may transfer incompletely, resulting in an aged, antique look. This additional element of texture can be appealing as well as useful for many kinds of projects too. Generally, cotton, poly-ester, and cotton/polyester blends are the easiest fabrics to work with, but experimentation will certainly lead to great discoveries. Finally, before using fabric, always wash and dry by machine and press, especially if the fabric will get wet or washed in the future.

Techniques and Tips
for Fabric Transfers

There are a variety of products specifically designed for fabric transfers, making it easy to achieve just about any look imaginable. Each method, of course, has its own advantages and disadvantages, so consider what quality is most important for the finished product. Some of these qualities include durability, matching the original image as closely as possible, translucency, and softness.

TRANSFER METHODS

HEAT TRANSFER PAPER

The easiest, fastest way to transfer images to fabric is with heat transfer paper. It takes three basic steps: print or copy the image onto the paper, cut away the excess, and iron it in place. There are many brands of heat transfer paper available, most of which offer translucent heat transfer paper, so the color of the fabric merges with the transfer. In all the white areas of the design, it will be the color and texture of the fabric that dominates. For this reason, white or light fabric colors often work best. Solid, dark-colored artwork, however, can be successfully transferred to dark fabrics. Also available are opaque heat transfer sheets, which can be transferred to any color fabric. All white areas of the design will remain pure white. The process is a little different from standard heat transferring, in that the transfer is peeled off of a backing sheet first. Once the transfer is positioned on fabric, a silicon pressing sheet, which is included with the paper, is used to safely iron the transfer in place.

Tips & Tricks for Heat Transfer Sheets

• The transfer will be a mirror image of the original—so don't forget to reverse the artwork when transferring or it will read backwards. Copiers have a setting for this, as do image-editing programs. This step isn't necessary, however, with opaque heat transfer paper.

• Use firm pressure and a circular motion to iron transfers in place. It should take only thirty seconds to a couple of minutes to adhere a transfer to fabric. (The finer the fabric the quicker the transfer.) Once the transfer has heated up, use lighter pressure with the iron because the transfer will be malleable and prone to smearing at this point.

• The manufacturer of a particular brand of transfer paper will usually have suggested settings for the iron temperature. Some, however, do not. Generally, use an appropriate setting for the type of fabric being used. If the transfer becomes cracked or crazed try a lower setting and iron for a shorter period of time. If the transfer doesn't seem to be taking very well, try a higher setting and iron for a longer period of time.

• Peeling a transfer when still warm yields a matte finish, while peeling a transfer when cool yields a shinier finish.

• Check if a transfer is complete by peeling up one corner. If it is still sticking to the backing paper in spots, simply iron the area again.

• Pay special attention to the edges of the transfer to be sure they are completely fused. These areas are often the most difficult.

- If an area of the transfer bubbles up or starts to peel after the backing is removed, just cover that area with a piece of the used backing (one that doesn't have any residual bits of transfer left on it) and go over the area again.

- Also note that fabric with transferred images, including printable fabric, is more resistant to pins and needles. Take this into consideration when sewing, and use a machine whenever possible.

PRINTABLE FABRIC

This specially coated, backed fabric can be used with ink jet printers and copiers. Both washable and nonwashable kinds are available, so be sure to check the package before purchasing. June Tailor's washable, colorfast Printer Fabric is a good choice, because it yields dependable results. The sheets are available in white and off-white. Printable fabric is fairly expensive, so always print on paper first to check for any problems with artwork. Then print on the fabric when the design is finalized.

Tips & Tricks for Printable Fabric

- Before printing, check for any bumps on the surface of the fabric and carefully pick them off. Often, these will come off after rinsing the fabric, and will result in a white spot if they aren't pulled off beforehand.

- Follow the manufacturer's directions for rinsing fabric to make it colorfast. Have dry, absorbent towels on hand as well. Press the rinsed fabric between the towels to squeeze out all excess water, then lay flat to dry. This helps prevent colors from bleeding, which can be especially undesirable if there is type in the design.

- Printable fabric will shrink anywhere from $1/8$" (3 mm) to $1/2$" (1 cm) after rinsing, so it's crucial to measure the fabric as you cut it, rather than depending on the image for sizing.

- Add a matching, colored border around the artwork for the seam allowance. It will also compensate for shrinkage and prevent any white from peeking through when piecing a project together.

LIQUID TRANSFER MEDIUM

This medium, which is available in clear and opaque formulas, creates a permanent and washable transfer. Simply brush the liquid on a photocopy, then place the paper face down on a piece of fabric and gently smooth it out with a sponge brush or by rolling the bottle of medium over it. Try not to apply too much pressure or the medium will ooze out from under the paper. The transfer then has to dry twenty-four to forty-eight hours, depending on humidity. Once dry, remove the paper backing by saturating it with a damp sponge, then rubbing it off.

Tips & Tricks for Liquid Transfer Medium

- An old credit card makes a great tool for applying the medium smoothly and evenly, with a minimum of effort.

- Leave a small tab or two of extra paper on the transfer when trimming it out to making handling and placing it on the fabric easier.

- Although liquid transfer medium works best with photocopies, ink jet printouts on photo-quality, matte-finish paper can also be used. Printouts tend to wrinkle when they absorb the medium, and these wrinkles cause the medium to dry in unattractive ridges. Try printout transfers no larger than 3" (8 cm) or 4" (10 cm) and with a thin coat of transfer medium, then place them immediately on the fabric to minimize this effect.

- When using liquid transfer medium, there is no need to worry about crazing or peeling, which can sometimes be a problem with heat transfers.

- Take into consideration that these kinds of transfers should not be ironed or dry-cleaned when planning a project.

Memory *Art Canvas*

A prestretched canvas is the perfect choice for creating a commemorative photographic compilation like this one, which chronicles the fun, romantic weekend one couple had in Venice Beach, California. So dig up all those vacation, party, or holiday photos and start photocopying or scanning them to make the perfect gift for friends and family. Liquid transfer medium is the best choice for stretched canvas, which is awkward to iron evenly. Also, color copies work best with this method. (Be sure to read *Tips & Tricks for Liquid Transfer Medium* on page 17 for more information.) To finish the project, try painting the edges of the canvas for a quick faux-frame.

MATERIALS

- *prestretched canvas*

- *clear liquid transfer medium*

- *craft knife or scissors*

- *sponge brush applicator*

- *large sponge*

Starting *Out*

Tinting photos in various, fun shades is easy to do with any image-editing program. Consult the application's guidebook for specific methods, or have a photocopy clerk adjust the hues.

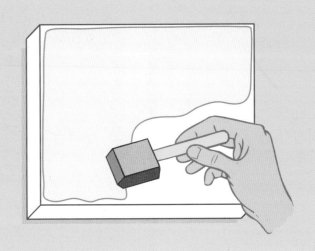

STEP 1

Prepare the transfers. Photocopy or scan and print out the photographs to be used. Play with the size and arrangement of the photos, and lighten or darken the images if necessary. The colors of the images can be manipulated with a copier or a computer (see page 10, *Modifying Art by Hand and Computer*). Next, get a color copy of the prepared artwork. If using an inkjet printer, use a high-quality matte-finish paper and the paper's corresponding setting for the printer. Then have a color copy made of the print out. Don't forget to flip the image, if desired. Let the paper dry for thirty minutes before proceeding.

STEP 2

Brush the medium on the canvas and adhere the transfer. Cut the transfer out along the edge of the image with scissors or a craft knife. The canvas used here is 8" x 10" (20 cm x 25 cm), so only one piece of paper was needed. For a larger canvas, tape together the pieces of paper on the reverse side. Be sure to align the seams carefully. Brush a thick, even coat of transfer medium on the canvas using a sponge brush applicator. The coat should be about 1/16" (1.5 mm) thick. Next, lay the artwork face down on the medium. Use a bottle or a brayer to gently smooth the transfer and press it into the medium. Let the transfer dry for twenty-four to forty-eight hours, depending on humidity.

[Tip:]

If the transfer doesn't cover the entire front of the canvas, apply the medium directly to the transfer while it is lying face up on a piece of wax paper or plastic wrap. Then, place the transfer face down on the canvas. Be sure to place tabs of paper on opposite sides of the image for easier handling.

STEP 3

Remove the paper transfer with a sponge. Moisten the entire transfer with a damp sponge and wait a few minutes for the water to saturate the paper. Then, use the sponge to rub the paper off the canvas using a circular motion. Let the surface dry. If there are any clouded areas, which indicate residual paper, rub the surface again with a damp sponge.

Variation:

Experiment with image-editing "filters" to modify a single photo. The watercolor filter in Adobe Photoshop Elements was used here for a painted look. For more tips on modifying art by computer, see page 11.

Commemorative *Collage Pillow*

The frame for this photo of my grandfather was made using various ID cards, which tell some of his life story and commemorate his many roles. Ordinary, old documents often have interesting graphic elements, and they confer history and lineage to a project. Approach the design of the pillow as a biographical journey to create an interesting, effective, and highly personal collage. Try using diplomas, birth certificates, passports, awards, or newspaper clippings of special events. Then, focus on the most important parts of each, like names, signatures, or seals, making sure they are highly visible in the collage. Before assembling the collage, adjust the value of the images so that they are similar by using a using a photocopier or a computer. This will create a unified design with a patterned effect.

MATERIALS

- *1 sheet of printer fabric*

- *½ yard (46 cm) of fabric for border and back of pillow*

- *14" x 14" (36 cm x 36 cm) pillow form*

- *straight pins*

- *needle and thread*

- *scissors or rotary cutter*

- *cutting mat*

- *clear ruler*

- *optional: sewing machine*

Starting *Out*

Before beginning the project, be sure to wash the fabric for the border and the back of the pillow to remove any residual chemicals from the manufacturing process.

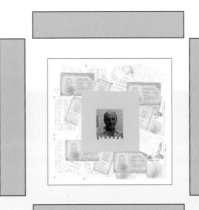

STEP 1

Prepare and print out artwork. Photocopy or scan and print out the photographs and items to be used for the collage. Play with the size and arrangement of the images (see page 10, *Modifying Art by Hand and Computer*). Make the final piece of art 8" (20 cm) square, then print it onto or have it copied to the fabric sheet. Trim the fabric so that there is a 1/4" (5 mm) white border around the image.

STEP 2

Assemble the pillowcase. Cut one piece of 14 1/2" x 14 1/2" (37 cm x 37 cm) fabric for the pillow back and four pieces of 3 1/2" x 14 1/2" (9 cm x 37 cm) fabric for the border. Next, center the border strips along each edge of the printer fabric and pin in place. The pieces will overlap at each corner. Stitch each border strip in place, starting and stopping 1/4" (5 mm) from the corners of the printer fabric. Press the seam allowances towards the printer fabric. Then, miter each corner. To do this, bring the outer edges of both border strips together, pin them in place, and mark a 45 degree angle extending from the corner of the printer fabric to the outer edge of the border strips. Sew along this line, then trim 1/4" (5 mm) from the seam. Press the seam allowances open.

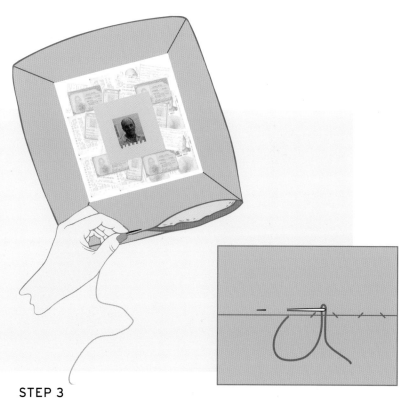

STEP 3

<u>Stuff and close the pillow</u>. Pin the pillow back to the pillow front,
right sides together. Stitch 1/4" (5 mm) from the edges of the pillow,
leaving an 8" (20 cm) opening at the bottom of the pillow for turn-
ing. Then, clip the corners diagonally to reduce bulk. Next, turn the
pillow cover right side out and insert the pillow form. Finally, slipstitch
the opening closed.

Variation:

Silky satin paired with a central pattern like this illustrated Chinese illustrated lotus, makes an elegant, easy
pillow. Most iron-on transfer sheets
will work well with 100 percent poly-
ester fabric, such as satin; check the
package for specific recommendations. Choose a light or white color
that won't obscure the transfer, and
be sure to hold the slippery fabric
taut and in place while ironing. Then,
assemble the pillow as described for
the main project, but use two pieces
of fabric cut to the same size. The art for
this project can be found on page 96.

Indian *Folk Art Bag*

The soft, natural colors of canvas and wood are perfect complements to the colorful, nature-inspired themes of the hand-painted Indian folk art used on this bag. A simple iron-on transfer is the best and easiest method for the smooth surface of canvas. Use transparent heat transfer paper so that the color and texture of the canvas blends with the artwork, enhancing the hand-painted feel. Try using a coarser, more open fabric such as jute or burlap for a rustic look. Also, remember to launder and machine-dry the bag before decorating. Any shrinkage in the fabric will damage the transfer.

MATERIALS

- *plain canvas tote bag*
- *heat transfer paper*
- *metallic fabric paint*
- *craft knife or scissors*
- *thin paint brush*
- *iron*

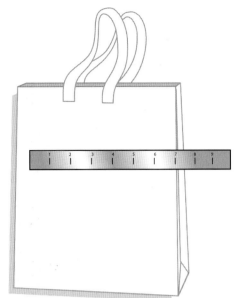

Starting *Out*

Try adding a simple, painted border around the transfer to accentuate the folk art motif. A linear border followed by a dotted border was used here for a traditional Indian textile look. The art for these projects can be found on page 96.

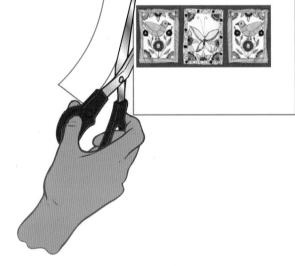

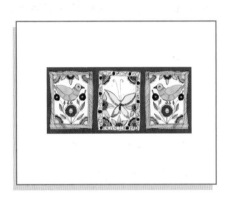

STEP 1

Prepare the transfer and the bag. Measure the tote bag to determine the how large the artwork needs to be. Then, photocopy or print the artwork onto a heat transfer sheet, following the manufacturer's instructions. Press out any creases in the tote bag and snip off any imperfections, such as nubs of fabric that may interfere with the transfer.

STEP 2

Cut out the transfer. Use scissors or a craft knife, a cutting mat, and a ruler. Cut as closely to the artwork as possible, without cutting into it.

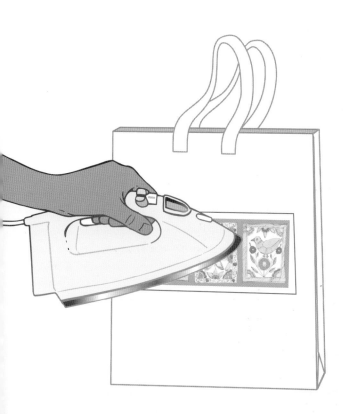

STEP 3

<u>Iron the transfer in place</u>. Again, follow the manufacturer's directions. A medium heat setting works best for transferring onto fabric. Tack the center of the transfer down first, then the edges. It will take thirty seconds to a minute to complete the transfer. Let the transfer cool for several seconds before checking to see if it has been completely transferred. If it resists peeling, then let it cool completely. Add a metallic hand-painted border if desired.

Variation:

Vintage luggage labels from the golden age of travel—that is, when people traveled by sea instead of by air—are works of art in their own right. Scatter a bunch on a tote bag for an instant world-traveler look. Use the same method described for the folk art bag to transfer the labels.

Indonesian *Table Runner*

Try using printer fabric to replicate beautiful patterns from antique fabric. Many clip-art books contain full-color photographs of actual fabrics, including details such as embroidered embellishments. Using these gorgeous, handmade designs will lend an air of sophistication and history to a project. The batik design used here makes a sumptuous runner when bordered with shiny, elegant black and silver fabric. Repeat the image as necessary to create a runner to fit any table. Then, add a simple border in a contrasting color to make the design pop out.

MATERIALS

- *printable fabric*

- *½ yard (46 cm) of black satin*

- *¼ yard (23 cm) of silver satin*

- *invisible nylon thread*

- *scissors or rotary cutter*

- *cutting mat*

- *clear ruler*

- *straight pins*

- *needle*

- *optional: sewing machine*

Starting *Out*

Determine how large the runner needs to be by beginning with the size of artwork cut from the printer fabric. Then, sketch out the design on a piece of graph paper to keep track of how many pieces of fabric are necessary to make the runner. The art for these projects can be found on pages 98 and 99.

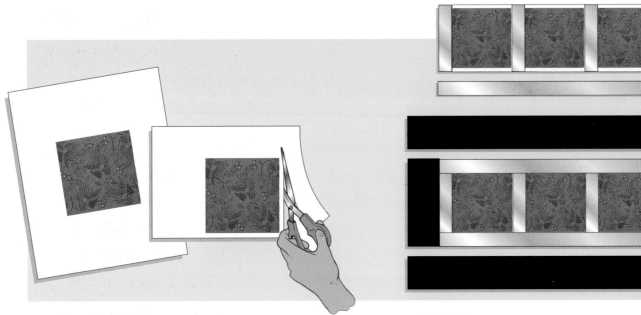

STEP 1

Prepare and print out artwork. Scan the art, making sure it is 8" (20 cm) square, then print it out on the fabric sheet following the manufacturer's instructions. Print as many sheets as needed for the runner. Be sure to read Tips & Tricks for Printable Fabric on page 17. Then, trim the fabric leaving a 1/4" (5 mm) white border around the image.

STEP 2

Make the runner top. Machine-wash and dry the satin, then press To make the 1" (3 cm) silver border, first cut 1 1/2" by 8 1/2" (4 cr x 22 cm) strips to separate each printer fabric panel. For the featur runner, which has three printer fabric panels, four separating strips are needed. Sew the panels together with a silver strip in between each, and on both ends. Press the seams open to flatten the piece panels. To complete the top and bottom of the silver border, cut tv strips measuring 1 1/2" (4 cm) wide by the length of pieced panel, and adding 1/2" (1 cm) for the seam allowance. Sew the strips inta place. To make the outer black border, cut two 3 1/2" by 8 1/2" (9 cm x 22 cm) strips and sew them to each short end of the piece panel. This will create a 3" (8 cm) wide black border when the rur ner is complete. To complete the top and bottom of the black bord cut two strips measuring 3 1/2" (9 cm) wide by the length of pieced pa adding 1/2" (1 cm) for the seam allowance. Sew the strips into pla

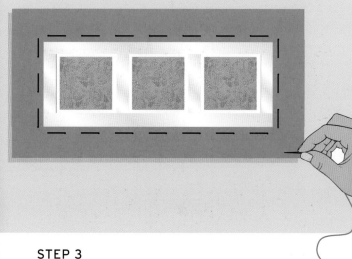

STEP 3

<u>Stitch the runner top and back together</u>. Measure the pieced runner top, and cut a piece of fabric for the back that is exactly the same size. Pin the runner top and back together about 1" (3 cm) from the edges, fronts facing. Then, stitch ¹/₄" (5 mm) in from the edges, using a sewing machine or a needle and thread. Leave an opening along one short end large enough to turn the runner right side out. Clip the corners diagonally to reduce bulk, then turn the runner right side out. Slipstitch the opening closed (see page 25).

Variation:

This easy-to-sew table runner can be made in an afternoon. It makes a light, airy accent to bring a bit of summer to any room. Plain, store-bought or antique linens are also perfect candidates for decorating with a few quick transfers. The butterflies here were made using pressed larkspur and rose petals. Try using other flowers or plants to personalize artwork for transferring. The variety of floral shapes and colors is sure to inspire creativity. First, press petals in a phone book until they are dry. Then arrange them on a piece of white paper using tiny dabs of glue to secure them. Then, photocopy or scan them to make transfers.

Transfers to Fabric **33**

~2000~

Livia & Isaac

Transfers *to Wood*

Wood provides a beautiful, functional, and readily available surface for transfers. Veneers, unfinished wood, and even finished wood can be decorated and enhanced with photos and artwork. There is even specialty veneer on the market that can be safely run through an ordinary ink jet printer. Most fabric-oriented methods of transfer can be used successfully on wood, and the finished project will look fantastic if a few key differences are taken into consideration. 🐾 The trick to a successful wood transfer is to coordinate the color and grain of the wood with the photo or illustration that is to be transferred. Generally, lighter-colored woods with simple or minimal grain patterns work best when the final image needs to remain as close to the original as possible. Darker or heavily grained woods will modify the image quite a bit, which opens up a whole realm of artistic possibilities that is bound to inspire interesting, expressive projects. When using transparent transfer mediums or papers, the beauty of the wood shows through in all the white areas of an image. This makes the transfer more convincing, and adds depth and sophistication to the project, such as in the frame project on page 38. 🐾 Seek out wooden surfaces in the home that are in need of refurbishing or decorating, such as end tables, chair backs, or shelves. By carefully selecting the image, transfer method, and surface, it's possible to create pieces that seamlessly blend the art with the object. Sometimes a small accent is all that's needed, and sometimes completely covering a surface is most effective. It's also a good idea to test ideas by trying them out on a piece of scrap wood that closely matches the color and grain of the intended transfer surface. Finally, don't forget to experiment with all kinds of wood as well as different types of artwork.

Techniques and Tips
for Wood Transfers

As with fabrics, there are a variety of transfer methods from which to choose when working with wood. In general, note that softer woods, such as balsa, take transfers more easily and quickly. Harder woods like oak will also work, but the process will take longer. It's also a little trickier, because the transfer can slip and smear once it is heated but not yet fully fused to the wood.

Always begin with finely sanded, unvarnished, unsealed wood. This will ensure that the surface is as porous and smooth as possible, which results in the highest quality transfer. Seal or varnish the project after the transfer has been adhered to protect both the wood and the artwork, but test the finish first. Some heavy-duty or industrial-strength finishes can damage transfers. Acrylic, water-based products are always a safe option.

TRANSFER METHODS

HEAT TRANSFER PAPER

Heat transfer paper is intended for transferring to fabric, but it can be applied to virtually any surface, including wood. To use it successfully on wood, there are a few things to keep in mind. Following are some troubleshooting tips and tricks (for further information on heat transfer paper and how to use it, see page 16).

Tips & Tricks for Heat Transfer Sheets on Wood

- Use gentle pressure and a straight, up-and-down motion to iron transfers in place. The transfer is more malleable and prone to smearing on wood than on fabric, so do not use a circular motion. Opaque transfer sheets are less apt to smear than translucent sheets.

- Translucent heat transfer sheets for copiers are easier to work with on wood than those designed for ink jets, which tend to slip and smear more.

- Use a medium to low heat setting for wood to avoid crazing. The wood will heat up quickly, but it will take longer than with fabric to transfer an image.

- Generally, wait until a transfer has cooled slightly to peel it. Otherwise, it will most likely tear off unevenly unless the wood is very soft, like balsa.

- If an area of the transfer bubbles up or starts to peel after the backing is removed, cover with a piece of the used backing and go over it with very light, quick strokes with an iron.

- Opaque transfer sheets work well with darker or heavily grained woods, because the integrity of the transfer remains intact. Painting around a transfer is another effective way to visually integrate it with the wood. This can soften the edges of the transfer and make it seem as if it has been hand painted.

PRINTABLE WOOD VENEER

This specially treated wood can be used with ink jet printers but not color copiers. It is also fairly expensive, so always print on paper first to check for any problems with artwork, then print on the veneer when the design is finalized. Once printed, it can be used the same way standard veneer would be used—for marquetry and other kinds of inlay, game boards, cards, candle shades, and just about anything else.

Tips & Tricks for Printable Wood Veneer

• Store the veneer in its protective package, and place it under a stack of books to keep it flat.

• Avoid touching the wood's surface before printing. Oils can interfere with the transfer process.

• Let the printed veneer dry for one hour before using it.

• To seal the wood, first use a spray finish to avoid smearing the ink. A brush-on finish can then be applied, if desired.

• Printers usually have a "thick mode" that can be engaged when printing on cardstock or other materials that are thicker than regular paper. Set the printer on this mode when using veneer.

• Load only one sheet of veneer at a time and no other papers. It's a good idea to load and eject a sheet before printing to check for any problems.

• If the edges of the veneer are damaged, this could interfere with the printer's ability to grab the sheet. Simply trim it to create a new, perfect edge, and keep in mind that there will be less space to print on when designing the transfer.

• This material is very absorbent, so fine lines have a tendency to bleed. Using a lot of ink, then, creates a blurry image. In general, try to use the least amount of ink possible to obtain acceptable results. Higher printing resolutions yield more detailed images, but they also use more ink. Try to find a balance between the two.

Border-Framed *Mirror*

This wide-edged frame is perfect for a transfer project because it offers a lot of room for artwork. Jazz up a plain, ordinary frame with a pretty, detailed border. There is a multitude of clip art books that offer an array of styles and colors from which to choose. The straight edges of the border here were a cinch to cut, but more intricate designs are well worth the effort. Both finished and unfinished frames will take transfers. Unfinished wood is easier to work with because the surface is more absorbent, but be sure to apply any paint or stains before adhering the transfer for a cleaner result. Before applying a transfer over a slick finish, do a test on the back of the object to make sure the result is acceptable. See page 36 for tips.

MATERIALS

- *wooden frame*

- *heat transfer paper*

- *tape*

- *craft knife or scissors*

- *iron*

- *ruler*

- *cutting mat*

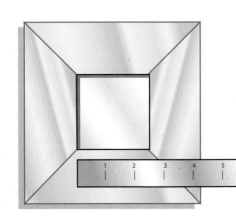

Starting *Out*

Do a test transfer on a piece of scrap wood of the same type as the frame before beginning the project to determine the optimal heat setting for the iron. The setting will vary from one brand of transfer paper to another. The art for these projects can be found on page 98.

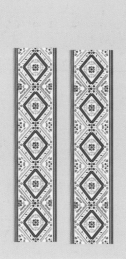

STEP 1

Prepare the transfer. Measure the frame to determine the size that the border needs to be. Then, scan or make four photocopies of the artwork at the necessary percentage. Create a continuous border by piecing together four strips of the artwork; this can be done by hand or on a computer. Next, photocopy the prepared artwork to a heat transfer sheet for color copiers by following the manufacturer's instructions.

STEP 2

Cut the transfer out. Use scissors or a craft knife, a cutting mat, and a ruler, and leave $1/16$"–$1/8$" (1.5 mm–3 mm) around the artwork. Next, use small pieces of tape to secure the two opposite sides of the transfer. This will help prevent it from sliding around the surface of the wood. Try to tape only the outer $1/16$"–$1/8$" (1.5 mm–3 mm) border of the transfer.

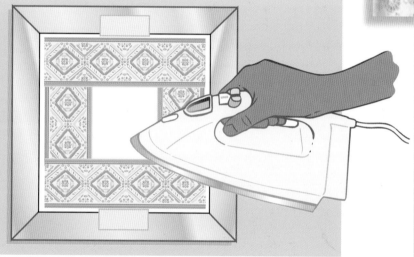

STEP 3

<u>Iron the transfer in place</u>. A medium to low heat setting works well for a finely finished wooden surface. Use a straight up-and-down motion when ironing rather than a side-to-side or circular motion, to prevent the image from smearing. It should take only a minute or two to complete the transfer. Let the transfer cool before peeling it off to ensure a complete transfer.

Variation:

Try adding a few smaller transfers to an unfinished wooden frame for quick accents. The black-and-white illustrations used here were colored with pencils before they were copied to a piece of heat transfer paper. To prepare the frame, coat it with translucent, white water-based wood stain and let it dry completely. Then, iron the transfers in place. It is not necessary to tape the transfer to secure it if the iron will cover all or most of the image at once. Finally, coat the frame with a colored water-based wood stain, if desired. Don't worry if some of the stain gets on the images, because it can be easily wiped away.

Illustrated *End Table*

The art nouveau-style illustration on this tabletop is surrounded by a painted border and stained wood for a matted, framed look. The painted border also helps to visually integrate the transfer with the surface of the table, while staining the other areas calls attention to the beauty of the wood. Pairing these decorating techniques creates the illusion of hand painting. This is especially the effect when opaque transfer paper is used, because detailed images are less apt to become muddled or obscured by inconsistencies or dark knots in the wood. Try refurbishing antiqued furniture with a few transfers, but leave the distressed finish intact.

MATERIALS

- *unfinished wooden table*

- *green pickling gel or water-based stain*

- *acrylic paint*

- *acrylic varnish*

- *opaque heat transfer paper*

- *craft knife*

- *sponge applicator brush*

- *ruler*

- *iron*

- *pencil*

- *masking tape*

Starting *Out*

Use masking tape for clean, crisp lines when painting the border. Don't worry about a clean inner edge, though, because the transfer will cover it.

The art for this project can be found on page 100.

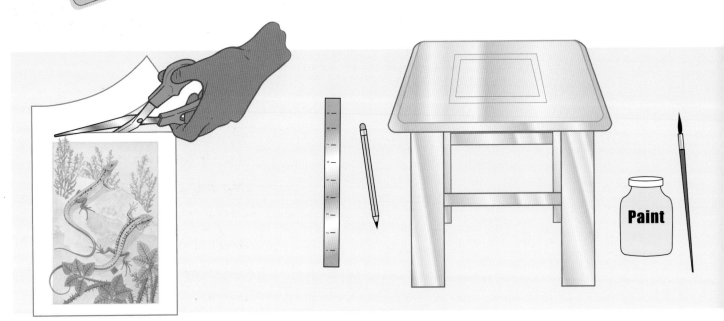

STEP 1

Prepare and print out artwork. Measure the tabletop to determine the how large the artwork needs to be. Then, photocopy or print artwork onto an opaque heat transfer sheet following the manufacturer's instructions. Leave the paper backing on the transfer and carefully trim around the tail and flowers that extend past the border of the art using a craft knife and cutting mat.

STEP 2

Stain and paint the table. First, mark the desired position of the artwork on the tabletop with a pencil and ruler. Then, measure and mark a border around the area to use as a painting guideline. Next, apply a water-based stain or pickling gel to the table with a sponge applicator brush, leaving the space for the artwork and painted border untouched. Cactus green pickling gel by Delta was used here. Once the stain is dry, paint the border with opaque acrylic paint.

STEP 3

Iron transfer in place. Preheat the iron on a medium heat setting. Peel the backing off the transfer and position the transfer on the table. Place the silicon pressing sheet over the transfer and use a circular motion and gentle pressure to adhere the transfer. This should only take a few minutes. Be sure all the edges of the transfer are secure. Once the transfer has cooled, finish the table with two or three coats of acrylic varnish.

Variation:

Try decorating the sides or the legs of a table instead of the top for a more understated look. Follow the directions for the main project, but completely paint and stain the table before applying the transfers. A white transparent stain was used for the tabletop, and the remaining areas were painted. Remember to mark pencil guidelines for each transfer to help in positioning. The art for this project can be found on page 101.

Faux-Painted *Clock*

The graphic, stylized floral design on this clock is reminiscent of the decorative folk painting often seen on wooden furniture. Simple, solid clip art like this is typically black to begin with, but solid colors can easily be changed. Even a basic image-editing program will have color-manipulation capabilities. If creating artwork using a copier, simply ask the clerk to change the hue. The monochromatic color scheme makes the clock easier to read, and it is easy to create with transparent transfer paper. As long as the transfer color is similar to the stain, the colors will merge and match well.

MATERIALS

- *unfinished wooden clock kit*
- *wood stain*
- *acrylic varnish*
- *heat transfer paper*
- *craft knife*
- *cutting mat*
- *sponge applicator brush*
- *fine sandpaper*
- *lint-free rag, such as a T-shirt*
- *iron*

Starting *Out*

Unfinished wooden clocks kits come with a movement and hardware and are very easy to assemble. Be sure to check if the clock hands are included or not. See *Resources* on page 112 for information. The art for this project and the variation can be found on pages 101 and 102.

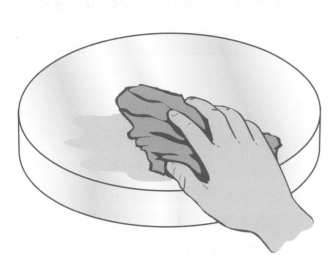

STEP 1

Stain the clock face. First, smooth out any rough spots with fine sandpaper. Remove all dust with a damp rag. Then, apply the wood stain. Purple oil-based wood stain mixed with an equal amount of white wood stain was used here to create a lavender patina. The clock face was also treated with an extra layer of pure white stain to make it a little lighter than the beveled edge. Wait at least twenty-four hours for the stain to dry before applying the transfer or it will be difficult to adhere.

STEP 2

Prepare the artwork. Measure the clock face to determine how large the artwork needs to be. Then, photocopy or print the artwork to a heat transfer sheet, following the manufacturer's instructions. Trim the artwork, removing as much of the white areas as possible.

[Tip:]

Oil-based wood stains take at least a day to dry completely, but their advantages are greater control and a finer finish. They are best applied with a lint-free rag, which eliminates the need to clean brushes with harsh solvents.

STEP 3

Iron the transfer in place. Preheat the iron on a low to medium heat setting. Use a straight up-and-down motion when ironing, rather than a side-to-side or circular motion, to prevent the image from smearing. This should only take a few minutes. Be sure all the edges of the transfer are secure, and check frequently to see if they are adhered. Let the transfer cool completely before peeling the backing paper off. Use a craft knife to cut the center of the transfer out, where the hole for the clock movement is located. Then, finish the clock with one or two coats of acrylic varnish. Once dry, attach the movement and hands to the clock face according to the package instructions.

Variation:

Try whitewashing wood to even out the variations when using intricate patterns. Some of the wood grain will still show through, but the transfer will remain distinct. A layer of white water-based wood stain, which dries in a few minutes, was applied to this clock. Be sure to apply this type of stain quickly and evenly. To determine the correct placement of the numbers for a clock face, use graph paper to easily but precisely divide the area into twelve segments, like a pie.

Giorgetta D'Marie

Livia McRee

Isaac Stone

Family *Tree*

This family tree is easily updated anytime there is a marriage or birth, because the photographic panels are a snap to make using inexpensive, easy-to-cut balsa wood. Arrange the panels on a wall to visually suggest a tree, or lay them out in a traditional genealogical pattern. Skeletonized leaves can be used in many ways to accent the panels and are available in several colors at craft and art supply stores. Also try using pressed foliage or flowers. To add names, first print them out from a word processing program, then have them reversed and copied to a heat transfer sheet at a copy shop.

MATERIALS

- *balsa wood planks*
- *skeletonized leaves*
- *decorative papers*
- *white pickling gel or water-based stain*
- *heat transfer paper*
- *craft knife*
- *cutting mat*
- *glue stick*
- *sponge applicator brush*
- *fine sandpaper*
- *iron*

Starting *Out*

Use a glue stick to quickly and easily adhere the paper and leaves to the photo panels.

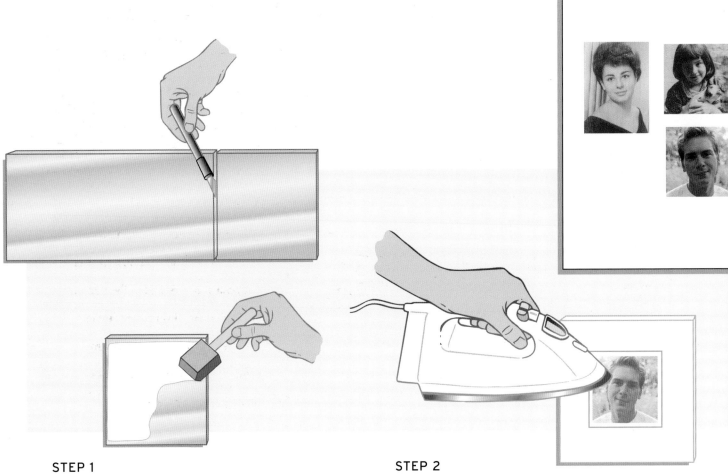

STEP 1

Cut and stain the panels. Cut the balsa wood planks into squares or rectangles. The ones here are 6" x 6" (15 cm x 15 cm) and 6" x 7" (15 cm x 18 cm). Smooth the cut edges with fine sandpaper. Then, apply a transparent white wash to the panels with a sponge applicator brush. Let them dry thoroughly for several hours or overnight; any moisture in the wood will prevent the transfers from adhering properly.

STEP 2

Prepare and iron the transfers in place. Compile the photographs to be used, then size them using a color copier or a computer. Photocopy or print artwork onto a heat transfer sheet, following the manufacturer's instructions. Fit as many as possible on each sheet. Carefully trim around each photo using scissors or a craft knife and cutting mat. Next, preheat the iron on a low to medium heat setting. Adhere the transfers to the centers of the panels. Use a straight up-and-down motion when ironing, rather than a side-to-side or circular motion, to prevent the image from smearing. This should only take a few minutes. Check adhesion frequently as you iron, and be sure all the edges of the transfers are secure. Let the transfers cool completely before peeling the backing paper off.

Variation:

Make panels to celebrate and commemorate special occasions, such as a special anniversary, family reunion, or graduation. Silver-coated leaves and metallic papers were used to complement the black-and-white photograph used here.

STEP 3

<u>Decorate the panels with leaves and paper</u>. Arrange and adhere the leaves as desired on the panels. Then, measure and cut squares of paper that are 1/2" (4 cm) larger all around than the transfers. Cut out the centers of these paper squares to create a 1/4" (5 mm) border for the transferred photographs. Position them over the transfers and adhere to the panel. To cover the edges of the panels, cut 6" (15 cm) strips; determine how wide the strips should be by measuring the thickness of the wood, then add 1/2" (1 cm). This will ensure a 1/4" (5 mm) border around the front and back of the panel. Lightly score the strips lengthwise, 1/4" (5 mm) in from both sides, using a craft knife. Fold the strips in to a *U* shape and adhere them to the edges of the panels. Finish the panels with a coat of water-based acrylic varnish, if desired.

Transfers *to Stone and Porous Surfaces*

Transfers can be applied to virtually any porous surface, which opens up an exciting realm of possibilities for the crafter. Terra-cotta, marble, plaster, stone—all these materials can be transformed with artwork and photos. From flowerpots to marble coasters, decorated clay and stone can be incorporated into the home with ease. Use plaster or other casting materials for custom-made surfaces ranging from molding boxes, frames, and ornaments, to just about anything else. The four projects in this section are merely a starting point and are intended to be an inspiring introduction to this fun way of crafting with images. When working with hard, porous surfaces, there are two important differences in the transfer process to keep in mind. Most importantly, it will take a longer time to adhere the transfer. In order for proper fusing to take place, the entire surface must be thoroughly heated—something that is more quickly achieved when using fabrics and wood. Also, once heated, the whole object will usually retain this heat for several minutes, especially stone surfaces, so wear protective gloves. Also, it may be difficult to get a complete transfer when a hard surface is bumpy or fairly uneven, since there is no give as there is with fabric and even wood. Try sanding the surface, if possible, or avoiding areas with pits or chips. Explore the variety of materials available at home-improvement centers and tile stores, because these places are sure to be full of potential craft projects. As long as a surface is fairly smooth and fairly porous, there's sure to be way to decorate it with transfers. It's easiest to transfer to a flat surface, but even rounded surfaces can work, so don't be intimidated by them. Finally, experiment with anything and everything—there's always a new technique waiting to be discovered.

Techniques and Tips *for Stone and Porous Surface Transfers*

The materials used in this chapter—stone, marble, plaster, and ceramics—come in many different colors and textures. Usually, these raw materials are sold for a particular use, but don't let that be a limitation. Flooring tiles, when backed with cork, make great coasters; garden slate, fitted with hanging hardware, can be used as a plaque; and inexpensive terra-cotta pots can be broken apart, decorated, and used in a mosaic.

After completing a few transfer projects, it will be easy to determine what types of surfaces will work. In general, flat, smooth, and porous surfaces are ideal. Curved surfaces are more difficult, but not impossible to transfer to. Nonporous materials like glass and metal could be used, but a much higher heat, such as that of a kiln, is needed for a successful transfer.

While no specific products exist—yet—for transferring to these types of surfaces, beautiful, durable, easy transfers are possible. Don't be afraid to improvise or use a standard technique in a new way. This often leads to surprising, satisfying results. As you get to know the different transfer methods and products available, it will become easier and easier to predict how a certain one will work on a given surface.

TRANSFER METHODS

HEAT TRANSFER PAPER

Both opaque and translucent heat transfer sheets can be ironed on stone and porous surfaces. Opaque transfers are very useful for medium- to dark-colored surfaces, such as terra-cotta and slate. See page 16 for a discussion of heat transfer paper and how to use it, but refer to the tips and tricks listed here for troubleshooting when working with the stone and porous materials used in this chapter.

Tips & Tricks for Stone and Marble Transfers

- For stone and marble, preheat the iron on high. It will take several minutes to complete the transfer, because the entire stone needs to become hot before the image will bond to it.

- Tack down the center of the transfer using firm up-and-down-pressure. Once it is stationary, vigorously iron the image using a circular motion.

- The image is only prone to smearing once the stone is completely heated, but at this point, the transfer should be complete. Check the progress frequently by using a craft knife or similar tool to lift up a corner of the transfer.

- Wear protective gloves when working with stone and marble, because they will become very hot during the transfer process. Also work on an appropriate surface that won't be damaged by the heat.

- For a finish ranging from matte to satin, peel the transfer backing off slowly, once it has cooled off enough to handle. For a glossier finish, wait for the transfer to cool completely before peeling.

- If there are any pieces of the transfer left on the backing, stop peeling and press it back into place. Then, reheat the area and let it cool completely.

- Sometimes, stone surfaces will have chips, cracks, or nicks. The transfer won't adhere to these areas that dip below the surface. Sometimes, this enhances the design by giving it an antique look. To fill the cracks for an even surface, use nonsanded white grout. Tint premixed grout with acrylic paint or grout powder with dry paint pigments.

Tips & Tricks for Ceramic Transfers

- Preheat the iron and set it on high, as with stone and marble. It will take several minutes to complete the transfer as well. Be sure to iron vigorously in a circular motion once the transfer is tacked down.

- Use only unglazed pottery, such as classic terra-cotta pots or bisqueware. Unglazed pottery will have a matte, chalky finish. Bisque is low-fired, usually white, and comes in a variety of forms, such as frames and vases. Purchase it from paint-it-yourself pottery studios or ceramic suppliers.

- Use coarse sandpaper to smooth any bumps, or use an industrial metal file for large bumps.

- Sponge off ceramic surfaces and let them dry completely before transferring. There is usually dust and fine clay residue on the surface of unglazed pottery. It may take several washings to get the surface totally clean.

- Since ceramics such as terra-cotta are dark, images on translucent heat transfer paper will be significantly modified by the color of the clay. A photograph, for example, will create a subtle pattern that appears to have faded over time. Dark, solid line images will create a stronger, more obvious pattern.

- To preserve the functionality of such an item as a flowerpot, seal the entire surface, including the interior. Unglazed ceramics are very absorbent, and contact with water will eventually damage transfers.

Tips & Tricks for Plaster Transfers

- Preheat the iron on a medium setting. It will take several minutes to complete the transfer, but if it isn't adhering well, turn the heat to high and iron more firmly and vigorously.

- There are many premade plaster shapes and forms available, which makes this material ideal for experimentation.

- Plaster objects are easy to make from scratch; simply measure out a portion of the dry mix, and slowly add water until a pancake batter consistency is achieved.

- Experiment with premade molds, or improvised forms such as cardboard boxes.

- Try tinting plaster with dry paint pigments before adding water.

Stone *Tile Coasters*

Artificial stone tiles, such as the ones used here, are inexpensive and are available at most home-improvement stores. Choose tiles with a smooth, evenly colored surface with a few hairline cracks or other imperfections for an antique, mural-like effect. Be sure the tiles are unglazed but highly polished, which creates an absorbent, smooth surface that is perfect for transfers. The vintage advertisements on these coasters might have been painted on a pub or restaurant wall, and using the transparent heat transfer method replicates this effect. And since heat transfers are designed to be functional fabric embellishments, they stand up well to hot drinks, moisture, and washing.

MATERIALS

- *4" (10 cm) stone tiles*

- *heat transfer paper*

- *cork or felt*

- *craft knife or scissors*

- *ruler*

- *cutting mat*

- *iron*

- *oven mitts*

- *permanent glue*

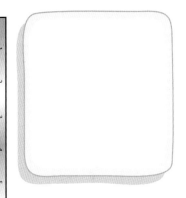

Starting *Out*

Stone tiles will heat up quickly when ironed, so wear oven mitts and be careful when handling them. The art for this project can be found on page 103.

STEP 1

Prepare and print out artwork. Select the artwork and determine the size it needs to be to fit the coasters. Square transfers will work best. Next, photocopy or print artwork to a heat transfer sheet, following the manufacturer's instructions. Be sure to flip the image if there is type so that it will read correctly when transferred.

STEP 2

Cut the transfers out. Use scissors or a craft knife, cutting mat, and ruler. Leave an $1/8$" (3 mm) border around the artwork.

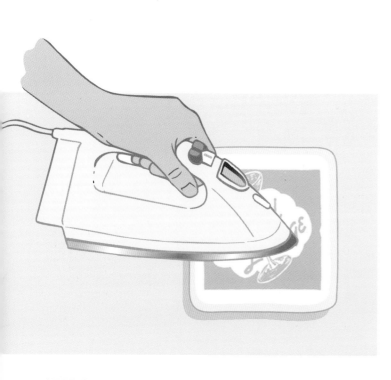

STEP 3

<u>Iron the transfers in place</u>. Follow the manufacturer's directions. A high heat setting works best for stone surfaces. Tack the center down first, then the edges. It will take several minutes to complete the transfer. Keep checking the edges to see if they have been completely transferred. Finally, adhere cork or felt to the back of each tile with permanent glue.

Variation:

These classic architectural illustrations are a perfect fit for white marble coasters. Black-and-white art works best with the grayish streaks that run through this stone, which otherwise tends to muddy and obscure color images. To work with marble, just follow the directions for the main project. The art for this project can be found on page 104.

Faux Porcelain *Plaster Box*

These plaster boxes can be made quickly and inexpensively using premade molds, but many household objects, such as Tupperware and cardboard boxes, can be used as molds too. The pure white, claylike finish of plaster can be used to convincingly replicate the look of porcelain. When combined with a blue and white Chinese pattern, the result is reminiscent of traditional decorative pottery. Translucent heat transfer paper fuses perfectly with plaster, while preserving the inherent, subtle tonal variations that add a realistic touch to the finished project. Try adding thin layers of high-gloss varnish until the box takes on a glazed look. Let each coat dry completely before applying the next for the most effective sheen.

MATERIALS

- *Quick-drying craft plaster*

- *heart box mold*

- *silver acrylic paint*

- *acrylic varnish*

- *heat transfer paper*

- *scissors*

- *sponge applicator brush*

- *paintbrush*

- *iron*

Starting *Out*

A wash of silver acrylic paint thinned with water was used on the edges and sides of this box for a subtle antique finish. Use silver foil sheets for a shiny, pure metallic look. The art for these projects can be found on page 104.

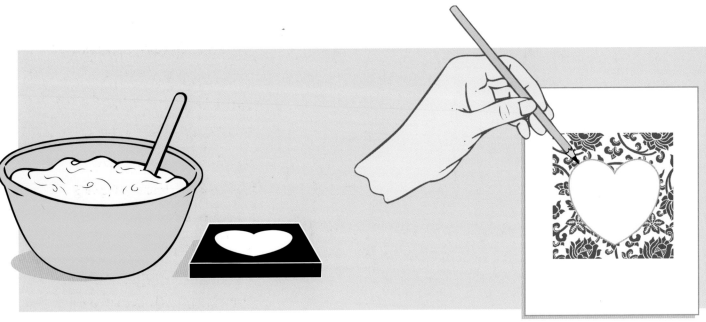

STEP 1

Make the plaster box. Following the manufacturer's directions, mix water into the plaster slowly until a consistency like that of pancake batter is achieved. Use a disposable container and a wooden stick. Then, pour the mixture into the mold and tap around the edges to bring air bubbles to the surface. Make sure the mold is on a level surface. Let it dry for about thirty minutes, until it is firm to the touch but still cool and damp. Then, remove the box and lid from the mold and either air dry for twenty-four hours or quick-dry using a microwave according to the manufacturer's instructions. Paint the sides and edges of the box if desired.

STEP 2

Prepare the artwork. Photocopy or print artwork onto a heat transfer sheet following the manufacturer's instructions. Make sure the artwork will be big enough to cover the box lid. Then, trace the box lid shape on the back of the transfer using a pencil (the outline of the artwork should still be visible). Cut along the traced line with scissors.

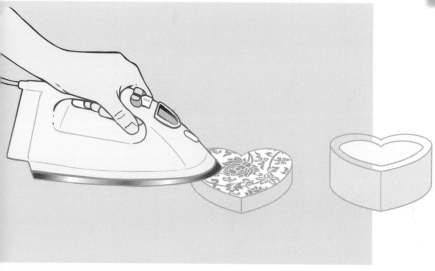

STEP 3

Iron the transfers in place. Preheat the iron on a medium to high heat setting. Place the transfer face down on the box lid and iron using a circular motion and firm pressure to tack it down. Once it is in place, continue ironing it until it is completely adhered, using gentle pressure to avoid smearing it. This should take several minutes. Once cooled, peel away the paper. Finally, finish the entire box with one or two coats of acrylic varnish using a sponge applicator brush.

Variation:

An ornate transfer can transform a simple, plain container into a treasure box, perfect for gift giving or storing precious jewelry. Size a square piece of art to fit perfectly on the lid, and follow the directions for the main project. (Plaid makes several different kinds of molds for plaster, including the square design seen here. See *Resources,* page 112, for further information.)

Terra-Cotta *Pots*

Unglazed terra-cotta makes an interesting, practical surface for transfers. When selecting pots, keep in mind that the smoother they are, the easier it will be to transfer images. The flat, angled sides of this pot made the transfer process even easier, and the rectangular shape of each side lends an Egyptian air to the project. Delineating the top, bottom, and each side edge accentuates the cartouche effect. This design can be translated to any pot by simply painting rectangular borders around a stack of three or more transfers like the bird used here.

MATERIALS

- *unglazed terra-cotta pots*

- *yellow ochre acrylic paint*

- *acrylic varnish*

- *opaque heat transfer paper with silicon pressing sheet*

- *craft knife*

- *cutting mat*

- *sponge applicator brush*

- *paintbrush*

- *iron*

Starting *Out*

Opaque transfer paper takes easily to the often rough, rounded, and uneven surface of terra-cotta. Sealing the pot's exterior with varnish makes it a functional piece, but to further protect the transfers from moisture, coat the inside as well with terra-cotta tile sealer (available at home centers). The art for these projects can be found on page 105.

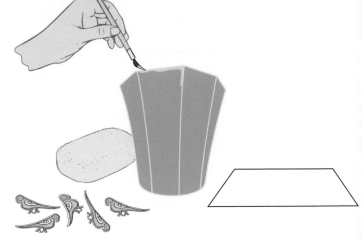

STEP 1

Prepare and cut the transfers out. Determine how many images will be needed to decorate the pot. Then, photocopy or print the artwork onto an opaque heat transfer sheet following the manufacturer's instructions. Fit as much artwork as possible on each sheet. Using scissors or a craft knife, a cutting mat, and a ruler, cut as close to the artwork as possible, without cutting into it. Leave the backing paper on while cutting.

STEP 2

Prepare and paint the pot. To prepare the pot, use a damp sponge to wipe away all dust and dirt. Then, add painted accents if desired. The edges of this octagonal pot were delineated to accentuate the vertical, Egyptian-inspired design.

STEP 3

Iron the transfers in place. Preheat the iron on a medium to high heat setting. Peel the backing off one of the transfers and position it on the pot. Next, place the silicon pressing sheet over the transfer and iron using a circular motion and gentle pressure to adhere the transfer. This should only take a few minutes. Be sure all the edges of the transfer are secure. Repeat with the rest of the transfers. Once the pot has cooled, finish the pot with one or two coats of acrylic varnish using a sponge applicator brush.

Variation:

A quick accent, like this floral artwork, is a fast and satisfying way to enhance ordinary pots. Try making several pots and placing them in a row along a sunny windowsill. Opaque transfer paper is the best choice for this project, because, unlike transparent transfer paper, it adheres well to rounded surfaces. Follow the directions for the main project to make these pots. Because they are round, however, they will need to be held stationary to keep them from rolling around while ironing the transfers in place. So be sure to wear an oven mitt on one hand.

Saltillo *House Number Plaque*

Made in Mexico, Saltillo clay tiles are similar to terra-cotta, but they have beautiful yellow, orange, and tan variegations—no two are alike. They are available from home-improvement centers and stores specializing in tile and flooring materials. The friendly sun pattern here accentuates the warm feeling of the tile and gives the project a south-of-the-border flair. The color of the artwork can be easily adjusted to suit a particular color scheme; try repeating a smaller version of the design in a very light color to create a more subtle background pattern.

MATERIALS

- *unglazed Saltillo tiles*

- *light yellow acrylic paint*

- *opaque heat transfer paper*

- *outdoor acrylic varnish*

- *craft knife*

- *cutting mat*

- *sponge applicator brush*

- *paintbrush*

- *iron*

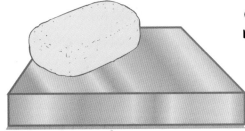

Starting *Out*

This plaque can be hung several ways. Try mirror clips or framing the entire tile in wood. A drill fitted with a masonry bit can also be used to make nail holes in the back of the tile. The art for these projects can be found on page 106.

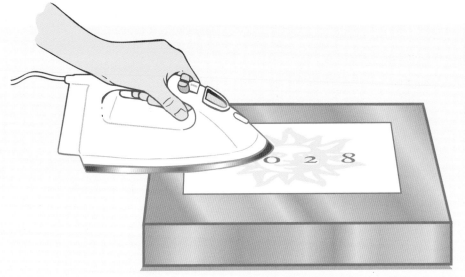

STEP 1

Prepare the artwork and the tile. Scan or copy the background to the desired size, and adjust the hue if desired. Then, choose a computer font for the house number. Some image-editing programs have typesetting capabilities. The type can also be set in a word processing program, then printed, scanned, and incorporated into the artwork as an image (see page 12, *Modifying Art by Hand and Computer*). Next, photocopy or print artwork onto an opaque heat transfer sheet following the manufacturer's instructions. To prepare the tile, use a damp sponge to wipe away all dust and dirt. Make sure the tile is completely dry before applying the transfer.

STEP 2

Cut the transfer out and iron it in place. Use a craft knife, cutting mat, and ruler. Cut as close to the artwork as possible without cutting into it. Leave the backing paper on while cutting. Preheat the iron on a medium to high heat setting. Peel the backing off the transfer and center it on the tile. Next, place the silicon pressing sheet over the transfer and with an iron use a circular motion and gentle pressure to adhere the transfer. This should only take a few minutes. Be sure all the edges of the transfer are secure.

STEP 3

Antique and seal the plaque. Combine one part of the yellow paint to two parts varnish to make a glazing medium. Apply the mixture with a sponge brush applicator over the whole tile for a sun-bleached look. Finally, finish the tile with several coats of acrylic varnish for outdoor use. Be sure to completely seal the tile for durability.

Variation:

Try using a full-color photo of the house, and superimpose the numbers on top as described in the main project. Rather than antiquing the entire plaque with a glaze, the photo seen here was lightened digitally to give it a softer look, which also helps to make the numbers pop. A color copier can also be used to lighten photos (see page 12, *Modifying Art by Hand and Computer*). Follow the directions for transferring the photo and sealing the plaque as described in the main project.

Transfers *to Polymer Clay*

Polymer clay is a versatile and inexpensive modeling material that readily takes transfers of many kinds. Available at craft-supply stores, it can be shaped easily and is then cured to a durable hardness in a home oven. There are many polymer clay tools and companion products, such as extruders to push molds, which make working with the clay even easier and more exciting.

All the standard transfer techniques can be applied to polymer clay, but this popular material has special properties that allow for even more ways to transfer images. Indeed, polymer clay is a material that sparks a lot of creativity and experimentation in those who are intrigued by its versatility. Black-and-white photocopies can be directly transferred to raw clay—no medium involved. Enhance the photocopy with colored pencils, and the pigments will also bake into the clay to create a permanent transfer. Also available is a liquid transfer medium called Liquid Sculpey, which can be used as a transfer medium with photocopies or be used to create decals that are applied to raw clay (see *Resources* on page 112). Polymer clay is available in a wide variety of colors, but use white, translucent, or lighter varieties when it is important to retain the color of the artwork or photo. Even so, there are many colors to choose from, including gorgeous pearlescent pastels. The many different colors, tools, and techniques of polymer clay craft are enticing, because there are so many possibilities for creating new and unique projects, from translucent suncatchers to decals that can be applied a to variety of surfaces. And with its flexibility to mold into anything, this is a perfect surface for transferring a treasured photo or a favorite illustration that can be created in an hour or less.

Techniques and Tips
for Polymer Clay Transfers

Polymer clay is simple to use, but there are a few things to keep in mind that will make the process even easier and more successful. First, work on a totally clean surface free of lint, oil, or dust. This debris will be picked up by the clay and is not only unattractive but also can cause incomplete transfers. Wear latex gloves to further prevent the clay from becoming soiled or oily. It's also a good idea to have a baking sheet set aside specifically for polymer clay. Though it is a nontoxic material, it's best not to reuse equipment used for curing clay to prepare food.

The projects in this section involve rolling out the clay to flatten it, which provides the ideal surface for transfers. In order to keep the thickness of the clay consistent, use craft wood sticks that are as thick as the clay needs to be. Simply tape them to the sides of the baking sheet and make sure the rolling pin's edges rest on the sticks while the clay is being flattened in the middle. Wood sticks are available in a variety of thickness at craft and hobby shops, from $1/16$" (1.5 mm) to $1/4$" (5 mm) and even thicker.

Finally, one essential tool for polymer clay crafting is the tissue blade, which is an extremely sharp, thin tool that makes cutting much easier. Tissue blades don't pull or push the clay as they cut, so the result is a nice, clean edge. Be sure to cut the clay once it's had a chance to firm up after the necessary initial kneading and shaping. Craft knives with new blades will also work well, but are much smaller than tissue blades, so more cuts will be needed to do the same amount of work.

TRANSFER METHODS

HEAT TRANSFER PAPER

Both opaque and translucent heat transfer sheets can be used on polymer clay. Both can be ironed on or baked on raw clay. See page 16 for a discussion of heat transfer paper and how to use it, but refer to the tips and tricks listed here for troubleshooting when working with polymer clay.

Tips & Tricks for Heat Transfer Sheets on Polymer Clay

· Place translucent transfers face up on the baking sheet, then put the raw clay shape over it. This helps the transfer adhere evenly and keeps it from buckling up during the baking process.

· Burnish translucent transfers with the back of a spoon after taking them out of the oven to ensure a good bond. Then, wait for the clay to cool completely before removing the backing.

· Opaque transfers can be baked on top of clay, rather than underneath, because they will stick firmly to the raw clay.

· Opaque transfers can also be applied to clay right after baking, when it is still hot.

· Do not bake the transfers more than once or longer than required to cure the clay, because they will start to shrink and crack.

DIRECT PAPER TRANSFERS

Photocopies can be applied face down on raw polymer clay, then baked. Black-and-white copies made from a black-and-white copier work best. When a color copy is used, only part of the ink transfers, resulting in very different colors. For example, black from a color copy machine can result in a rose color. This can lead to some interesting effects, but for truer color, enhance a black-and-white copy with good quality color pencils.

Tips & Tricks for Direct Paper Transfers on Polymer Clay

• In addition to photocopies, printouts from laser printers can also be used to make transfers, but those from ink jet printers cannot.

• The copy should be fairly dark to ensure a rich, solid transfer.

• If the transfer isn't working well or is coming out too light, try another copy machine or change the toner in the laser printer.

• Once the transfer is in place, try not to move the clay or the paper, because this can cause the image to smear. For this reason, it's best to work directly on a baking sheet.

• To create a transfer for a round surface, follow the normal procedure for flat surfaces, but leave the transfer on the clay for fifteen minutes, and don't bake it. Be sure to burnish it well. Then, remove the paper, carefully mold the clay into the rounded shape, and, finally, bake it. This is a great method for making beads.

LIQUID POLYMER TRANSFER MEDIUM

Liquid polymer transfer medium is available in transparent and opaque formulas. Any type of photocopy can be used to make a liquid polymer transfer, and they can be enhanced with color pencils. Just brush a layer of the medium directly on the image, then bake according to the manufacturer's directions. The resulting decal can then be peeled off the paper and used in a number of ways. To transfer to raw clay, just coat the clay with the medium and place the paper transfer on top, then bake as usual. (For information on availability see Polymer Products in *Resources* on page 112.)

Tips & Tricks for Liquid Polymer Transfer Medium

• Ink jet printouts made using standard or multipurpose paper will not create a transfer. However, using photo-quality, matte finish ink jet paper will create a perfect transfer with colors more vibrant than a color copy transfer.

• If the transfer is coming out too faint, try making a color or black-and-white copy darker, using a more brightly colored or darker image, or using a different copy machine altogether.

• Add color to the medium by mixing it with oil paints or dry pigment powders. Acrylic paint, which is water based, will create a bumpy texture during baking when the water boils off.

• After baking, if the transfer is hard to peel off, soak it in some water. The decal will not be damaged.

• When transferring directly to raw clay, be sure there are no air bubbles caught between the paper and the medium. Burnish the transfer with the back of a spoon, and wait until all the paper darkens. This indicates that the medium has soaked in thoroughly.

• The medium can be used as an adhesive to bond raw clay to raw clay, or raw clay to baked clay. Use only a thin coat to attach the pieces, then bake them. Too much medium will cause the pieces to slip and slide.

Pendant and Pin *Set*

This jewelry is made using photocopies of black-and-white illustrations and faux-stone polymer clay. The simulated rose quartz, jade, and turquoise clay featured here are just a few of the styles of specialty clays available. Only simple jewelry-making techniques and minimal supplies are needed to assemble the necklace and pin. Just check the bead and findings section of any craft-supply store. Try using a black-and-white photo and transfer it to brightly colored clay for a fun, contemporary necklace. Or, use miniature cookie cutters to create pendants with interesting shapes.

MATERIALS

- *polymer clay*

- *jump ring*

- *necklace chain*

- *pin backing*

- *silver paint*

- *¼" (5 mm) thick craft wood strips, at least 12" (30 cm) long*

- *rolling pin*

- *cookie sheet*

- *sharp craft knife or tissue blade*

- *pliers*

- *eye pin*

- *varnish*

- *permanent adhesive*

- *small paintbrush*

- *fine sandpaper*

Starting *Out*

It's best to use black-and-white copies for this project. Color copies create pale transfers, and the final color of the transfer will be completely off from the original. The art for these projects can be found on page 107.

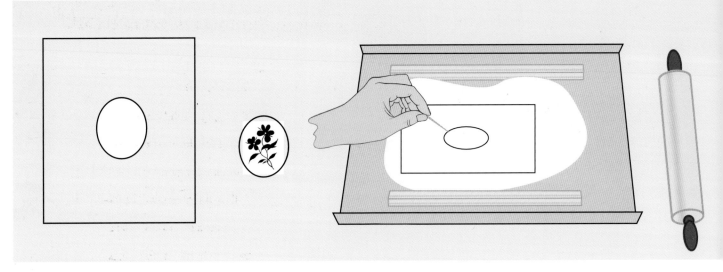

STEP 1

Prepare the artwork. Cut an oval or other shape from a piece of white paper to make a template of the pendant and pin shape and size. Lay it over the image to be used, then determine if the image needs to be enlarged or reduced to better fit the space. Photocopy the image at the appropriate percentage on a black-and-white copier, then cut out the image. Reverse the image when copying it, if desired.

STEP 2

Shape and bake the polymer clay. Knead a small handful of clay until it is softened and very pliable. Place the 1/4" (5 mm) wood strips on the cookie sheet so that the rolling pin rests on them and there is ample space in between to roll out the clay. When the clay is 1/4" (5 mm) thick, place the paper template on top and gently trace the outline into the clay with a craft knife, toothpick, or similar tool. Then, remove the template and carefully cut out the pendant shape with a tissue blade or sharp craft knife. Next, lay the photocopied image face down on the clay. Press it gently into the clay by going over it with the rolling pin once. Rub the edges gently to smooth them out, then stick an eye pin into the top of the pendant. Follow the same procedure to make the pin, but don't add an eye pin. Bake the clay on the cookie sheet following the manufacturer's directions, generally fifteen minutes per 1/4" (5 mm) of thickness at 275 degrees Fahrenheit (135 degrees Celsius).

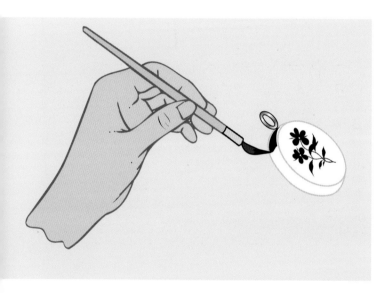

STEP 3

<u>Paint the pendant and pin</u>. Lightly sand the edges of the pendant and
pin if necessary to smooth the surface. Glue the pin backing in place
using permanent adhesive. Paint the edges and back of the pendant
with silver paint. Finally, finish with a coat of varnish, if desired.

Variation:

Try using a solid black
image on glitter or pearlescent clay for a bolder look.
Follow the directions for the
main project, but use black
paint to highlight the edges
of the clay. Use a jump ring
to connect the key chain's
eye pin to the key ring.

Tiled *Backsplash*

These nature-themed tiles make a serene and soothing accent to a room. Use them on walls or on furniture, such as a tabletop. The tiles can be directly applied to a surface or to a plank of wood to create an easy-to-handle inset. Or, border the plank with strips of painted wood as seen here, and use it as is. Rather than using cement grout, use polymer clay mixed with sand, which won't damage the tile surfaces. Finish with several coats of polymer clay gloss varnish for a glazed ceramic look.

MATERIALS

- *white polymer clay*

- *colored polymer clay for grouting*

- *sand*

- *rolling pin*

- *cookie sheet*

- *¼" (5 mm) thick craft wood strips, at least 12" (30 cm) long*

- *Translucent Liquid Sculpey (TLS)*

- *sharp craft knife or tissue blade*

- *wood carving V-gouge*

- *wood carving flat chisel*

- *sponge applicator brush*

- *palette knife*

- *varnish*

- *fine sandpaper*

Starting *Out*

Wood carving tools work wonderfully with polymer clay and can be used to create a variety of effects. For this project, a flat chisel was used to smooth and even out the edges of the tiles quickly and easily. The art for these projects can be found on pages 108 and 109.

STEP 1

Prepare the artwork. Photocopy or print out the artwork to be used. Next, cut out the artwork, trimming as close to the images as possible. Make sure color copies are deep and rich. For ink jet printouts, use photo-quality paper and print the images on the setting suggested by the paper manufacturer. This is essential—printouts on regular paper will not transfer at all, but photo-quality paper yields an even better transfer than a color copy. (For more on preparing images, see the Tips & Tricks on page 11.)

STEP 2

Shape and bake the polymer clay. Knead a handful of clay until it is softened and very pliable. Place the 1/4" (5 mm) wood strips on the cookie sheet so that the rolling pin rests on them and there is ample space in between to roll out the clay. When the clay is 1/4" (5 mm) thick, place the transfer on top and gently trace the outline into the clay with a craft knife, toothpick, or similar tool. Then, remove the transfer, cut along the line, and remove the excess clay without disturbing the tile form. Next, brush a layer of liquid polymer transfer medium over the clay, then lay the transfer face down on the medium. Go over the surface lightly with the rolling pin once. Bake the tiles on the cookie sheet for no more than fifteen minutes at 275 degrees Fahrenheit (135 degrees Celsius). Wait for the tiles to cool before removing the paper.

STEP 3

<u>Grout the tiles</u>. First, use a woodcarving gouge or similar tool to make shallow grooves in the back of each tile to aid adhesion. Next, lay the tiles down in the desired arrangement. Use sandpaper or a flat woodcarving chisel to trim the edges if necessary. To install, use strong, permanent glue. Next, knead a handful of polymer clay until soft and pliable to make grout. If desired, blend in sand for a more authentic look. The grout used here is a mixture of beige clay, translucent clay, and pale yellow sand. Smear the grout into the cracks between the tiles and smooth using a palette knife. Wipe away any excess on the tile surfaces. Then, bake again for 15 minutes at 275 degrees Fahrenheit (135 degrees Celsius).

Variation:

The advantage of using polymer clay to make tiles is the workability of the material and the speedy curing time. Virtually any image can be transferred to polymer clay with minimal color alteration. The coffee bean artwork on these tiles was made by colorizing a black-and-white photograph. See *Modifying Art by Hand and Computer* on pages 10–13 for more information.

Matisse *Kitchen Magnets*

Several coloring books are available from Dover Publications that are based on great paintings, spanning different periods and styles (See *Resources* on page 112 for ordering information). The magnets here are versions of Matisse paintings: *The Dream*; *Blue Nude I*; and *Nuit de Noël*. When coloring the images, keep in mind that bolder lines indicate black areas of the painting. The thinner guidelines indicate areas of the same color. Both colored artist's pencils and pastel pencils can be used. Look at art history books for inspiration to see the original colors of the paintings.

MATERIALS

- *white polymer clay*

- *colored pencils*

- *magnet tape*

- *¼" (5 mm) thick craft wood strips, at least 12" (30 cm) long*

- *rolling pin*

- *cookie sheet*

- *scissors*

- *sharp craft knife or tissue blade*

- *fine sandpaper*

Starting *Out*

For a rich, dark transfer, press firmly when coloring the photocopy to get lots of pigment on the paper. For a light wash of color, press lightly. The art for these projects can be found on page 110.

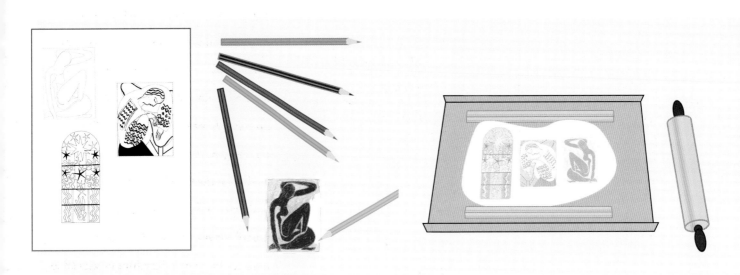

STEP 1

Prepare the artwork. Photocopy the artwork at the appropriate percentage on a black-and-white copier. The images supplied on page 110 are reversals of the original paintings. Next, color the images with pencils. Trim the artwork out, leaving an 1/8" (3 mm) border of white around the image.

STEP 2

Shape and bake the polymer clay. Knead a small handful of clay for each magnet until it is softened and very pliable. Place the 1/4" (5 mm) wood strips on the cookie sheet so that the rolling pin rests on them and there is ample space in between to roll out the clay. Roll the clay out until it is 1/4" (5 mm) thick, then place the transfer face down and press it gently into the clay by going over it with the rolling pin once. Cut around the transfers using a craft knife or tissue blade. Rub the edges gently to smooth them out. Bake the magnets on the cookie sheet following the manufacturer's directions, generally fifteen minutes per 1/4" (5 mm) of thickness at 275 degrees Fahrenheit (135 degrees Celsius). Once cool, remove the paper.

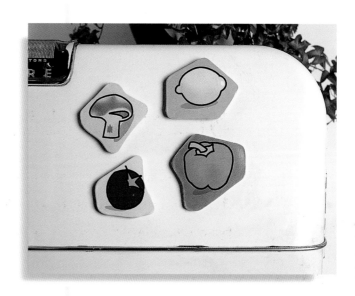

STEP 3

Apply the magnet backing. Cut off an inch or two (3 cm–5 cm) of the magnet tape, remove the paper backing, and adhere it to one of the magnets. Repeat for each magnet, and add additional magnetic strips if necessary for larger magnets. Apply one or two coats of varnish to seal the magnets, if desired.

Variation:

These retro-inspired magnets make a fun, colorful addition to any refrigerator. Opaque heat transfer paper was used here for a crisp, unbroken image with virtually no color change. Simply bake it directly on raw clay, rather than ironing it on. And since the transfer is opaque, bright or dark-colored clay can be used without modifying the artwork. Use clay that matches the color of the fruit or vegetable for an easy bordered look, or just paint the edges of the finished magnets. Try using the same image at various sizes to make a whole "bunch" of tomatoes, peppers, mushrooms, or lemons. Be careful not to bake the magnets longer than recommended by the manufacturer. The ideal length of time, fifteen minutes, is sufficient to complete the transfer. Any longer may cause it to wrinkle unattractively.

Suncatcher *Mobile*

These suncatchers are made of translucent polymer clay, which glows beautifully when bathed in light. The key to maximizing translucency, without sacrificing durability, is to roll the clay out to $1/8$" (3 mm) thick. Choose artwork that is brightly colored, with minimal, if any, white areas. For a striking display, make several mobiles of various lengths and stagger along a sunny window. For temporary hanging, use clear suction cups. For a more permanent solution, try screwing eye hooks into the top of the window frame.

MATERIALS

- *translucent polymer clay*

- *rolling pin*

- *cookie sheet*

- *$1/8$" (3 mm) thick craft wood strips, at least 12" (30 cm) long*

- *translucent liquid polymer transfer medium*

- *embroidery floss or thread*

- *acrylic paint*

- *varnish*

- *fine sandpaper*

- *sharp craft knife or tissue blade*

- *eye pin*

- *small round brush*

- *sponge applicator brush*

Starting *Out*

Be sure there are no air bubbles caught between the clay and the paper transfer. Wait for the transfer medium to soak into and darken the paper, which should reveal any areas that aren't making contact. The art for these projects can be found on page 111.

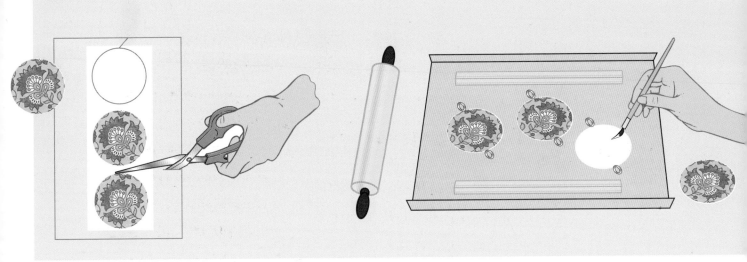

STEP 1

Prepare the artwork. Photocopy or print out the artwork to be used. Next, cut out the artwork, trimming as close to the images as possible. Make sure color copies are deep and rich. For ink jet printouts, use photo-quality paper and print the images on the setting suggested by the paper manufacturer. This is essential—printouts on regular paper will not transfer at all, but photo-quality paper yields an even better transfer than a color copy.

STEP 2

Shape and bake the polymer clay. Knead a small handful of clay until it is softened and very pliable. Place the 1/8" (3 mm) wood strips on the cookie sheet so that the rolling pin rests on them and there is ample space in between to roll out the clay. When the clay is 1/8" (3 mm) thick, place the transfer on top and gently trace the outline into the clay with a craft knife, toothpick, or similar tool. Then, remove the transfer, cut along the line, and remove the excess clay without disturbing the suncatcher form. Insert eye pins that have been trimmed to about 1/4" (5 mm) in length at the top and bottom of each suncatcher. Next, brush a layer of liquid polymer transfer medium over the clay, then lay the transfer face down on the medium. Go over the surface lightly with the rolling pin once. Bake the clay on the cookie sheet following the manufacturer's directions for baking the transfer medium. Bake no more than fifteen minutes at 300 degrees Fahrenheit (150 degrees Celsius).

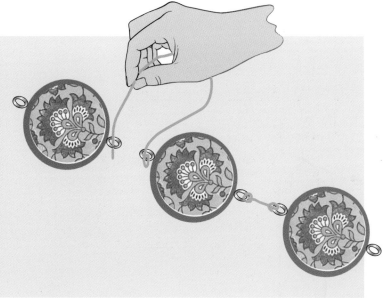

STEP 3

<u>Assemble the mobile</u>. Once the suncatchers are cooled, peel the paper off to reveal the transfer. Then, paint the edges, if desired. Apply a coat of varnish to each suncatcher. String them together using lengths of embroidery floss or invisible nylon thread.

Variation:

Suncatchers can be made in any shape. Experiment with different finishes for the edges as well. Silver foil tape, used by stained glass artisans as a base for leading, covers the edges of these suncatchers. Also try gilding foil, ribbon, or paper.

Gallery *of Art for Projects*

The copyright-free artwork used in this book can be found on the following pages. It is shown here at full size, according to the actual sizes used in the projects for this book. Photocopy or scan the art to make the projects in this book, and try modifying the sizes and colors to suit a variety of other craft and home decorating applications. When scanning images, set the resolution at 150 (dots per inch), which is ideal for both quality and speed. For more information, see *Modifying Art by Hand and Computer,* on pages 10–13.

LOTUS PILLOW, PAGE 25

INDIAN FOLK ART BAG, PAGE 26

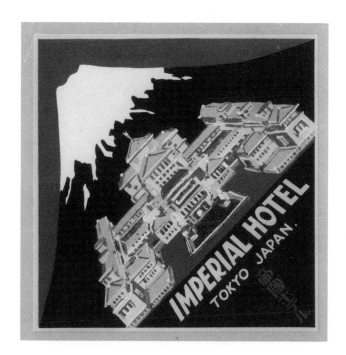

VINTAGE LUGGAGE LABELS, PAGE 29

BUTTERFLY TABLE RUNNER, PAGE 33

WOODEN FRAME WITH BIRDS, PAGE 41

BORDER-FRAMED
MIRROR, PAGE 38

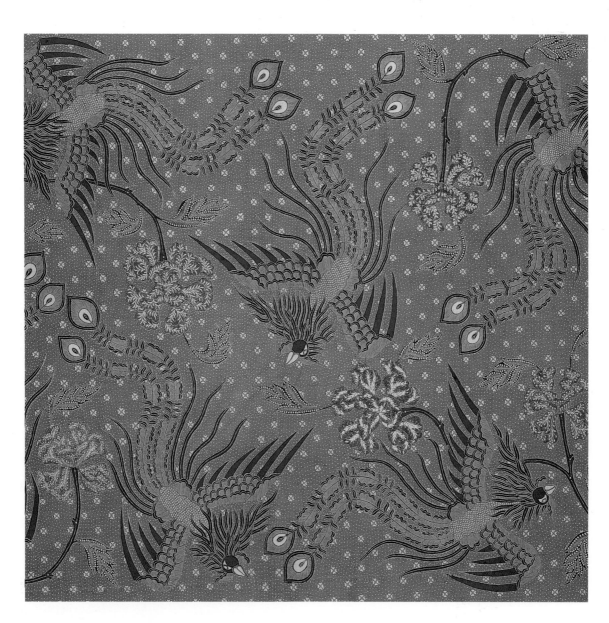

INDONESIAN TABLE RUNNER, PAGE 30

ILLUSTRATED END TABLE, PAGE 42

END TABLE VARIATION, PAGE 45

FAUX-PAINTED CLOCK, PAGE 46

0 1 2 3 4 5 6 7 8 9

WHITEWASHED CLOCK VARIATION, PAGE 49

STONE TILE COASTERS, PAGE 58

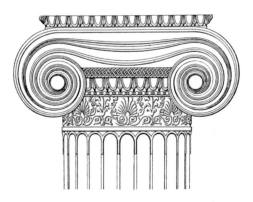

WHITE MARBLE COASTERS, PAGE 61

FAUX PORCELAIN PLASTER BOX, PAGE 62

SQUARE TREASURE BOX, PAGE 65

TERRA-COTTA POTS, PAGE 66

O I 2 3 4
5 6 7 8 9

SALTILLO HOUSE NUMBER PLAQUE, PAGE 70

PENDANT AND PIN SET, PAGE 78

KEYCHAINS, PAGE 81

TILED BACKSPLASH, PAGE 82

COFFEE BEAN TILES, PAGE 85

MATISSE KITCHEN MAGNETS, PAGE 86

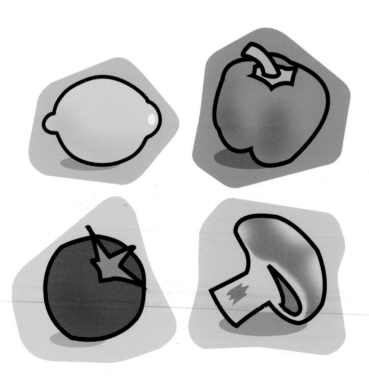

FRUIT AND VEGETABLE MAGNETS, PAGE 89

SUNCATCHER MOBILE, PAGE 90

SILVER-EDGED SUNCATCHERS, PAGE 93

Resources

The following mail-order resources offer a variety of traditional as well as unique craft supplies, including some of the harder-to-find materials used in this book.

Art Direction Book Co., Inc.
456 Glenbrook Road
Glenbrook, CT 06906
phone: 203-353-1441

The Art Direction Book Co. publishes books on graphic design and the Scan This Book clip art series.

The Art Store
4004 Hillsboro Pike
Nashville, TN 37215
phone: 800-999-4601
Web site: http://www.artstoreplus.com

The Art Store sells supplies for the professional and amateur, including canvases, varnish, and tools.

D. Brooker & Associates
Rt. 1, Box 12A
Derby, IA 50068
phone: 641-533-2103
fax: 641-533-2104
e-mail: dbrooker@dbrooker.com
Web site: http://www.dbrooker.com

D. Brooker & Associates manufactures several unique wood products, including the ink jet printable wood veneer.

Dover Publications
Customer Care Department
31 East 2nd Street
Mineola, NY 11501-3852
fax: 516-742-6953
Web site:
http://store.doverpublications.com

Dover Publications offers a staggering array of clip art books with themes ranging from cigar box labels to Japanese design motifs. Request a free catalog of clip art titles by going to the Web site or writing to the above address.

Fire Mountain Gems
28195 Redwood Highway
Cave Junction, OR 97523-9304
phone: 800-423-2319
e-mail: questions@firemtn.com
Web site:
http://www.firemountaingems.com

Fire Mountain Gems sells everything necessary for making jewelry, including semiprecious beads, handmade glass beads, silver and copper beads, wire, findings, and tools.

HobbyCraft
(stores throughout the United Kingdom)
Head Office
Bournemouth
phone: 01202 596100

HobbyCraft sells supplies for the professional and amateur.

John Lewis
(stores throughout the United Kingdom)
Head Office
Oxford Street
London W1A 1EX
phone: 020 7269 7711
Web site: http://www.johnlewis.com
John Lewis sells supplies for the professional and amateur.

June Tailor
P.O. Box 208/2861 Highway 175
Richfield, WI 53076
phone: 262-644-5288; 800-844-5400
fax: 262-644-5061; 800-246-1573
e-mail: customerservice@junetailor.com
Web site: http://www.junetailor.com
June Tailor manufactures transfer papers and washable, colorfast printer fabric. Call, write, or e-mail for retailer information.

Pearl Paint
308 Canal Street
New York, NY 10013
phone: United States order,
800-221-6845 x2297;
international, 212-431-7932 x2297
Web site: http://pearlpaint.com
Pearl Paint is a great resource for general art and craft supplies, including metal leaf in several colors, spray adhesive, and tools.

Plaid
P.O. Box 2835
Norcross, GA 30091
phone: 800-842-4197
Web site: http://www.plaidonline.com
Plaid manufactures Faster Plaster, a quick-drying craft plaster used in the heart box project on page 62, as well as molds for creating a variety of plaster objects perfect for transfer projects. Visit the Web site or call to order products or to get retailer information.

Polyform Products Co.
1901 Estes Avenue
Elk Grove Village, IL 60007
phone: 847-427-0020
Web site: http://www.sculpey.com
Polyform Products manufactures Sculpey brand polymer clay, and Liquid Sculpey, a liquid polymer transfer medium. Visit the Web site for tips, free projects, retailer locations, and polymer clay links.

TransferMagic.com
P.O. Box 190
Anderson, IN 46015
phone: United States, 800-268-9841;
international, 765-642-9308
fax: 765-642-9308
e-mail: info@transfermagic.com
Web site: http://www.transfermagic.com
TransferMagic.com manufacturers just about everything needed for transferring, including the ink jet Transfer to Dark paper used for several projects in this book. They also carry kits and tools for transferring to a variety of surfaces.

Walnut Hollow Farm, Inc.
1409 State Road 23
Dodgeville, WI 53533
phone: 800-950-5101
Web site: http://www.walnuthollow.com
Walnut Hollow Farm offers unfinished wood items, including frames, shelves, trays, and boxes. They also sell everything necessary for clock making, which can be purchased separately or in kits.

For Grandpa—

I miss you. Love, Stringbean

About *the Author*

Livia McRee is a craft writer and designer. Born in Nashville, Tennessee, and raised in New York City by her working-artist parents, Livia has always been captivated by and immersed in folk and fine arts, as well as graphic design. She now lives in California.

She is the author of two additional books, *Quick Crafts: 30 Fast and Fun Projects* and *Instant Fabric: Quilted Projects From Your Home Computer.* She has also contributed to numerous other books, including *Mosaics Inside and Out; The Right Light; Ceramic Painting Color Workshop;* and *Simple Elegance.*

Acknowledgments

I would like to thank the following people, who were all an integral part of creating this book:

Mary Ann Hall, who always gives me the best opportunities; Lorraine Dey, the awesome illustrator; Maryellen Driscoll, my very talented friend and editor; everyone at Rockport Publishers, especially the art director, David Martinell, and the photographer, Bobby Bush; my parents, for helping me find artwork and family photos; and to Brewster, my two-month old kitten, for helping me type the manuscript.

Special thanks to Biz Stone—for creating the fruit and vegetable artwork used in the 1950s kitchen magnets, and for his support and feedback, which is so essential to my creative process.